A ZEN FOREST

A ZEN FOREST

SAYINGS OF THE MASTERS

Translated by Sōiku Shigematsu
Foreword by Gary Snyder

WHITE PINE PRESS • BUFFALO, NEW YORK

Publication of this book was made possible, in part, with public funds from the New York State Council on the Arts, a State Agency.

First Edition

Library of Congress Control Number: 2004109161

Published by
White Pine Press
P.O. Box 236
Buffalo, New York 14201
www.whitepine.org

To the memory of Asahina Sōgen Rōshi

Contents

FOREWORD

The Mohave Indians of the lower Colorado River put all the energy they gave to aesthetic and religious affairs into the recitation of long poetic narratives. Some of the epics are remarkably precise in describing the deserts of the southwest, but the raconteurs held that they were all learned in dreams. By another sort of inversion, the world of Zen (Ch'an) Buddhism with its "no dependence on words and letters"—and unadorned halls, plain altars, dark robes—created a large and very specialized literary culture. It registers the difficulty of the play between verbal and non-verbal in the methods of the training halls. The highly literate Zen people were also well acquainted with secular literature, and they borrowed useful turns of phrase from any source at all, to be part of the tool kit, to be employed when necessary, and often in a somewhat different way. A final step was the sifting of Ch'an texts, Chinese poems and proverbs, Buddhist sutras, and Taoist and Confucian classics one more time. This was done in Japan in the sixteenth and seventeenth centuries, and the result was the *Zenrin Kushū*, "Phrases from the Zen Forest." Most of the phrases gathered are from Chinese poetry, so that R. H. Blyth could say that the *Zenrin Kushū* is "the Zen view of the world on its way through poetry to haiku."

Give this book a glance. It's not quite like any collection of quotations or selections from "great literature" that has been seen before. Eichō Zenji, who did the basic editing, and his successors knew what they were looking for. Soiku Shigematsu's introduction tells about that.

But the *Zenrin Kushū* selections could not have the terse power and vividness they do, were it not for the richness of the parent material. First, the terseness. It's all from Chinese. The Chinese language is mostly monosyllabic, with word-order grammar, and can be very economical. There is a long-established culture-wide delight in sayings and quotes, and there is a special lore of ambiguity and obscurity that plays on the many homonyms in the language. Early books such as the *I Ching* and the Taoist essays abound in "dark sayings."

The Zen phrase anthologies do not draw on deliberately obscure sayings, tongue-twisters, traditional riddles, and the like. With the exception of quotes taken from the texts of their own school, they present us with selections from the public body of sayings and quotes. Poems are never quoted whole, so that in this case the obscurity (especially for the Western reader) is from the absence of context. When the

Zen phrase is actually an old proverb, such as:

> To sell dog meat,
>   displaying a sheep's head.

several levels of meaning are instantly clear. In Chinese this would literally be: "Hang sheep head sell dog meat." Another proverb that comes into the phrase book is:

> One who flees
>   fifty steps
> Sneers at the other
>   who's done a hundred.

English is a relatively parsimonious language, but the Chinese for this is literally "Fifty steps sneer him ahead one hundred." The context is running away from battle.

The most common type of Zen phrase is the couplet borrowed from poems of five characters to a line. There are 578 such couplets in the Baiyō Shoin edition of the *Zenrin Kushū*. (Mr. Shigematsu has done away with the traditional arrangement of Zen phrases by number of characters. His original and personal sequencing makes the book easier to read straight through.) Seven-character lines, both single and paired, make up the next largest body of quotes, also from poetry.

Chinese poetry takes the crisp virtue of the language and intensifies it a turn again. It is also the one area of the literature where personal sentiment—vulnerability, love, loneliness —is to be found in an otherwise dry and proper terrain. The very first doctrine of Buddhism that Chinese intellectuals took to heart, in the fourth and fifth centuries A.D., was that of Impermanence. It fit well with the political experience of the times, the troubled Six Dynasties. The lyric poetry of that era is also full of woe and gloom. So almost from the beginning *shih* poetry has had a line to Buddhism. The Chinese (and almost everyone else) consider the T'ang poetry of the eighth century to be the crown of their literature. The poems of this period, infinitely superior to the weepy Six Dynasties lyrics, are the ones most often raided for Zen quotes. T'ao Ch'ien is a notable exception. We are speaking especially of the poets Wang Wei, Li Po, Tu Fu, Han Shan, and Liu Tsung-yüan. Although some were Buddhists, this does not matter to a Zen phrase. The power of image and metaphor, the magic of poetry, not ideology, is what counts. Contemporary with these poets were the great creative Ch'an masters Shen-hui, Nan yueh, Ma-tsu, Pai-chang, and Shihtou. For whatever reason, the Golden Age of Chinese poetry is also the Golden Age of Ch'an. Twelfth-century Ch'an masters who gathered and edited koan books out of the anecdotes and lives of T'ang masters were also reading and quoting the T'ang poets.

Many of the poems from which the Zen editors plucked quotes have been widely known by almost all Chinese and educated Japanese for centuries now. Some of them have entered the territory of *su hua,* or "common sayings," such as Tu Fu's:

The country is ruined: yet
  mountains and rivers remain.
It's spring in the walled town,
  the grass growing wild.

The context here is the destruction of the capital during the An Lu-shan rebellion. Tu Fu was not a Buddhist, yet his way of being and working came close to the essence. Burton Watson says of Tu Fu: "Tu Fu worked to broaden the definition of poetry by demonstrating that no subject, if properly handled, need be unpoetic.... There is evidence to suggest that he was versed in the lore of herbs and medicinal plants, and perhaps this knowledge gave him a special appreciation for the humbler forms of natural life. Some of his poems display a compassion for birds, fish, or insects that would almost seem to be Buddhist-inspired. Whatever the reason, he appears to have possessed an acute sensitivity to the small motions and creatures of nature.... Somewhere in all the ceaseless and seemingly insignificant activities of the natural world, he keeps implying truth is to be found."

The poets and the Ch'an masters were in a sense just the tip of the wave of a deep Chinese sensibility, an attitude toward life and nature that rose and flowed from the seventh to the fourteenth century and then slowly waned. The major Ch'an literary productions—*Wu-men Kuan, Ts'ung-jung Lu, Pi-yen Lu, and Hsü-t'ang Lu*—are from the twelfth and thirteenth centuries. It was a second Golden Age of Ch'an and another era of marvelous poetry, one in which many poets were truly influenced by Ch'an. The most highly regarded Sung-dynasty poet, Su Shih, was a Ch'an adept as well as poet and administrator.

> Valley sounds:
>   the eloquent tongue—
> Mountain form:
>   isn't it Pure Body?

This is part of a poem by Su Shih. The Japanese master Dogen was so taken with this poem that he used it as the basis for an essay, *Keisei Sanshoku*, "Valley Sounds, Mountain Form." Sung-dynasty Ch'an had a training system that took anecdotes and themes from its own history and lore and assigned them as subjects of meditation. The tradition that emphasized this, the Rinzai sect, is also called the Zen that "looks at sayings." The complementary school called Sōtō which cut down on the use of old sayings, is also called "silent illumination Zen." They were both brought from China to Japan on the eve of the Mongol invasions. Japan inherited and added on to its own already highly developed sense of nature the world view of T'ang and Sung.

Robert Aitken Rōshi has described koans (and by implication the "phrases from the Zen forest") as "the folklore of Zen." Borrowed in part from the folklore of a whole people, their use as Zen folklore is highly focused. These bits of poems are not simply bandied about between Zen students as some kind of in-group wisdom or slangy shorthand for larger meanings. They are used sparingly, in interviews with the teacher, as a mode of reaching even deeper than a "personal" answer to a problem; as a way of confirming that one has touched base with a larger Mind. They are not valued for the literary metaphor, but for the challenge presented by the exercise of actualizing the metaphor in the present. They help the student bring symbols and abstractions back to earth, into the body. Zen exquisitely develops this possibility —yet it's not far from the natural work of poems and proverbs anyway. Someone has said proverbs are proverbs because they are so true.

So if Zen has koans for folklore, the world has folklore for koans. Proverbs and short poems the world around are of like intensity and suggest equal depths. Though Mr. Shigematsu has chosen to eliminate the Zen phrases under four words long from his collection, it helps to know how they work and why. What would be the power of a one-word Zen phrase? I think of Harry Robert's account of Yurok Indian upbringing: If one did something foolish, all that Elder Uncle had to say was, "Well!" and a youngster would go off to ponder for hours.

Let us lock eyebrows with the seventh-century B.C. Greek poet Archilochos, a mercenary soldier:

> —Into the jug
>   Through a straw
>   *(translated by Guy Davenport)*

A Bantu riddle:

> A black garden
> With white corn
>   the sky and stars.

and the Philippines:

> The houseowner was caught;
> the house escaped
>   through the window
>   —Fish net.

and the Koyukon of the Alaskan Yukon:

> —We come upstream
> in red canoes
> the salmon.
>   (translated by Richard Dauenhauer)

and the Hawaiians:

> —Not all knowledge is
> contained in your dancing school.

and finally the people of Kentucky:

> "My feet are cold" one says

and the legless man replies:
"So are mine.
So are mine."

(Wendell Berry)

But beyond the fascinating Ch'an/Zen and world folklore
implications of this collection, it stands on its own as a kind
of "poem of poems." We can read Mr. Shigematsu's excellent
translations and follow his creative sequencing with an avail-
ability that has been earned for us by the modernist poetry
of this century. Let this book be read for the enjoyment of
the far-darting mind, and skip for the time any notions of
self-improvement. It is a new poem in English, winnowed out
of three thousand years of Chinese culture, by some of the
best minds of the East. It's also the meeting place of the
highest and the most humble: the great poets and the "old
women's sayings," as proverbs are called. Arthur Smith,
speaking of mandarin officials of nineteenth century China,
said they were "well known to spice their conferences and
their conversations with quotations from 'the old women' as
naturally as they cite the *Four Books.*"

For this book to exist, the Ch'an masters of the past, the
poets of the twentieth century, and the old women must have
joined hands.

—Gary Snyder

INTRODUCTION

A word is a finger that points at the moon. The goal of Zen students is the moon itself, not the pointing finger. Zen masters, therefore, will never stop cursing words and letters.

> A phrase
>   completely to the point:
> The eternal
>   donkey hitching post.

Abusive expressions are found everywhere in the writings of Zen masters.

   The essential principle of Zen is illustrated in the following sayings:

> Teaching
>   beyond teaching;

No leaning
on words and letters.

Point straight
at the mind;
See its nature
and become Buddha!

Zen experiences are not to be explained with words and letters. Only

The man who's
drunk water
Knows if it's
cool or warm.

Exactly!
Words
fail.

Nevertheless, many masters have left voluminous records. Why? Why did they leave so many "words" even against their own principles? This is certainly a contradiction. Indeed, Zen is paradoxical in every respect.

Careful examination of the phrase I quoted first provides a clue to this question. The point is that however wonderful an expression may be, it will be a stake that binds you unless you keep yourself free from it. Once this fact is fully understood, words and letters are not to be forsaken as good for nothing. On the contrary, they are quite important in that they help us to know what to avoid and what to do to attain true *satori*. And they are the only way to universalize and eternalize human experiences.

Thus, Zen masters find that the best way to express the unexplainable is to put their *satori* experiences in symbolic verse. In describing what cannot be expressed, there is no choice but to rely on symbolism. In this aspect, verse is indeed akin to Zen. Anyone who has once gazed with awe at the round, round moon can grasp it by the mere suggestion of a pointing finger. This is the very reason why the masters composed *satori* poems on many occasions during their lives.

Especially important poems for them may fall into one of the following two categories. One is to *tōkinoge*, or poems in which they depict symbolically the moment of satori; the other is the *yuige*, or final farewell poem for their disciples, in which their whole Zen experience is condensed. Together with these poems, their sermons were posthumously compiled by their disciples into a *goroku* (word record). Zen history books and koan collections were also compiled and published.

Against their own preachings, in this way many Zen masters made use of words, which as a result have become a very important element in Zen. Paradoxically, these words have brought about many memorable encounters beyond the realm of time and space.

The two mirrors
reflect each other.

> Arrowhead and arrowhead
> hit one another.

It is these word records that have linked the great Zen masters in different ages. These encounters are in some cases evidenced by the later masters' practice of devising *jakugo* (capping words, or brief Zen comments) for their forerunners' records.

Hekiganroku (The Blue Cliff Records), for example, is a typical case of *jakugo*. First, Setchō Zenji (Hsueh-tou, *980-1052*) compiled *Hyakusoku-juko* (One Hundred Koans with Verse Comments). A century later, Engo Zenji (Yuan-wu, *1063-1135*) added his introductions and prose commentaries to the koans and comments and "capped with words," to show his own view of each phrase or sentence in Setchō's book. The original koans, with the various additions by Setcho and Engo, were later compiled by the latter's disciples and called *Hekiganroku*.

For instance, one of Setcho's verses goes:

> A thousand peaks,
> winding, overlapping,
> look like indigo.

Engo's *jakugo* to it is:

> They're all Manjusri himself.
> Haven't you seen him?

In Japan, this *jakugo* exercise has been regarded as an important element of traditional koan study. Even today every student of the koan is expected to keep on hand at least one copy of the two major Zen *jakugo* handbooks: *Zenrin Kushū* (A Zen Forest Saying Anthology) and *Zudokko* (The Poison-Painted Drum).

Zenrin Kushū has its origin in *Kuzōshi* (A Saying Book), compiled in the late fifteenth century by the Japanese master Tōyō Eichō Zenji (*1428-1504*). This collection was later enlarged by Ijushi (nothing is known about him) and published in *1688*. Over the centuries, many different editions have been printed, sometimes with a slightly changed title or sometimes with different entries.

The *Zenrin Kushū* contains about six thousand Zen words, phrases, and verses mostly taken from various Zen classics, sutras, and the poetry of T'ang and Sung China. The entries are arranged into twelve sections according to the number of Chinese characters, from one character to parallel eight characters (sixteen characters). In no section, however, is any intended order found. They are arranged at random, scattered with no clear organization. This may have had some significance in Zen training, but it must have caused students a good deal of trouble. Every anthology of this kind today, therefore, has been edited in some order to meet the convenience of readers.

In the days of stricter discipline, under the guidance of their foster priests all pupils had to memorize each saying in this book before they could enter monastery life. This obligation was so burdensome for them that it has often been said: "Saying-book learning, three years—torture to every novice."

Zudokko is a two-volume handbook edited by Genro Fujita (*1880-1935*). It contains many essential sutras and classics of Zen. The first volume was published in *1916*. The second, *Zudokko: Zokuhen*, appeared in *1922*. Its last section is given to a saying collection called "Zudokko Kushū." This anthology section was compiled in the same style as that of *Zenrin Kushū* and contains more than *2,400* entries, but quite a few are common to both.

In koan study, the *rōshi* (master), after having examined the students from various viewpoints, orders each of them to submit appropriate *jakugo* for the koan. The students are required to express their own views of the koan in sayings chosen from these handbooks. Pulling out copies from the sleeves of their robes, they turn the pages repeatedly, trying to find the perfect saying from among the thousands of entries. In most cases, however, the novices will read in the lavatory or under shimmering candlelight at night, because reading is not openly allowed in monastery life.

In fact, this *jakugo* exercise helps the students to understand their own koan experiences more distinctly and deeply. They are thus sure to have a more clear-cut view of the koan study they have undertaken. *Zenrin Kushū* and "Zudokko Kushū" have been in this way the essential companions to all Zen followers.

From these two handbooks, I have chosen and translated

the selections in this anthology. All, I feel, are basic, inspiring, and timeless: basic for the understanding of Zen and in frequent use by Zen followers; inspiring for people who wish to find and identify the true self; and modern, that is, in sync with the sensibilities of people in our time. I have left out those that require too much knowledge of Oriental legends and historical facts, and I have also cut out sayings of fewer than four characters. It is true that the shorter ones are essential in Zen, but their very brevity demands much additional explanation.

Needless to say, each entry without exception reveals some phase of *satori* and Zen life. I hope readers will find in this anthology some windows onto the Zen way of life: Zen Universality, Individuality, Vitality, and Radical Humanity for the coming new age. From among the sayings that stimulate and inspire your poetic imagination and religious insight, choose one and "cap" your life with it. Then, instead of the life of "a poor player that struts and frets his hour upon the stage," you will be sure to build your own world.

Fortunately, Zen is not dogmatism. Zen goes beyond everything—even itself.

> Be master of yourself
>   —everywhere:
> All you do
>   proves true.

ACKNOWLEDGMENTS

My gratitude goes first to Ciaran Murray. But for his help, this work might never have progressed beyond draft form.

It was Gary Snyder who encouraged me to publish my translations and who honors them here with his foreword.

I am very grateful to Kijū Shigematsu, my father and teacher and the abbot of Shōgen-ji Zen temple.

I wish to express my heartfelt thanks to all—in the ten directions and in the past, present, and future— who have helped me complete this book, and I also wish to present this collection of sayings to all who hoped, hope, and will hope to live in the Original Self, that is, in Zen.

Shōgen-ji temple, Shizuoka
February 1981

A Note on the Illustrations: The Ten Oxherding Pictures, here presented in a modern version by Gyokusen, illustrate the ten stages of development in Zen practice and have long been used by students of Zen. The calligraphy presented for selected entries was done by Kijū Shigematsu.

THE SAYINGS

A dumb man has eaten
    a bitter cucumber.

Bite your middle finger
    with your fist clenched.

On the saddle,
    no man;
Underneath it,
    no horse.

Saying "fire"
    won't burn your mouth;
Saying "water"
    won't drown you.

A piece of dust
    in the eye:
Illusory flowers
    dance wildly.

Each time you show it
    each time
        it's new.

One encounter:
    once and for all.

Cast a net at it, but
    it'll slip out;
Call it, but
    it won't turnits head.

Settle in a phrase
    the essence of Zen.

The first stem,
    the second, crooked;
The third,
    the fourth, slanting.

One click makes him
    forget everything.

One moon
    shows
        in every pool;
In every pool
    the one
        moon.

A word
    once spoken
Can't be caught
    by rapid horses.

The tree splits
    the spring wind
        in two—
Southern branches stretch
    to warmth;
        northern, to cold.

An inch of
   tortoise hair weighs
      seven pounds.

Shouldering the plank
   —till death.

Thunder rolls
   once:
      a clear wind rises.

One man's speech
   is a rapid stream;
The other's,
   simple and artless.

One true man
   of no rank.

One blind man
    leads many blind men
Into the fire hole
    hand in hand.

    Get all T'ang China
    aboard the ship
      of a single leaf.

One leaf, fluttering,
    tells of autumn
        over all the country.

Store the whole world
    in a grain
        of millet!
Boil
    mountains and rivers
        in a two-quart pot!

Between snipe and clam
    the fight doesn't stop:
Both fall into
    the fisherman's hands.

I'll explain in detail
    why Bodhidharma
    came to China:
Listen to the evening
    bell's sounds. Watch
        the setting sun.

Blue mountains
   after rainfall
      —much bluer.

Rain bamboos,
   wood pines:
      all preach Zen.

Covering one's ears
   to steal the tinkling bell.

Clasping its young,
   a monkey goes home
      behind the green peak;
Picking a flower,
   a bird lands
      in front of the blue cliff.

A parrot cries,
    "Green tea!"
Give it to him, but he doesn't
    know what it is.

Flowers
    speak most—
        the smiling eyes of the peach.

Flowers, opening,
    meet wind and rain;
Human life
    is full of partings.

Pity! This
    vessel
Meets
    no one to fill it.

The servant asks me
  its deepest
    meaning:
Smiling, I point outside
  the silk-curtained window
    —the autumn moon.

The sweet
  swordblade
    of a lady's smile
Shreds a man's heart
  inch
    by inch.

Lotus leaves round,
  round, more than
    mirror-round;
Holly leaves sharp,
  sharp, more than
    gimlet-sharp.

Pity! A man
    endlessly juggling
        the waves of the Buddha Sea
Finally
    falls in
        and dies.

Summer stove,
    winter fan.

Eyes wide, entering
    the boiling water
        —with dignity!

Open your mouth—
    instantly wrong;
Move your tongue—
    against the truth.

A cow in Huai-chou
    eats rice plants:
The stomach becomes full
    of the horse in I-chou.

Ash-sprinkled head,
    soil-smeared face.

One word—
   to a wise man;
One lash—
   to a bright horse.

Outside void,
   inside void,
     inside-outside void;
Void, void
   void, void
     finally all void.

Scratching where you itch,
   from outside the shoes.

No cold spot—
   in a boiling cauldron.

Bring back
    the dead!
Kill
    the living!
Look! Look!
    The last month ends!

This brimming wine
    in the golden bowl:
Don't hesitate—drink it
    to the last drop!

Call it—
    no answer;
Watch it—
    no form.

When cold,
    freeze him to the bone!
When hot,
    boil him to the marrow!

Quietly holding
    a sutra, leaning
        against the pine tree,
To ask, smiling, his guest,
    "Hi!
        Where are you from?"

An autumn cicada,
    sticking to the dry tree,
Cries and cries
    without moving his head.

When cold
    say cold;
When hot
    say hot.

Cold plum blossoms
  show Bodhidharma's
    exact intention:
One petal flutters
  west—
    another, east—

To open eyes wide, lying
  in the coffin.

Eyes level,
  nose vertical.

Sand in the eyes,
  clay in the ears.

Tortoise hair is long;
  hare horns, short.

掬水月在手
弄花香滿衣

Eat when hungry!
  Sleep
     when tired!

Dip up water—
  the moon lies in your hands;
Touch a flower—
  the fragrance fills your robes.

To bounce a ball
  on the rapids.

Need fire?
  Best strike a flint.
Water?
  Dig a well.

A train of rings
  of an earthworm,
    which one is true?

To feel the first rain
   after a long drought;
To come across an old friend
   in a foreign country.

To have no posterity
   for fear of mourning.

To move the mountain
   by scooping water;
To banish the shore
   by setting sail.

A cornered rat
   will bite a cat;
A fighting sparrow
   will attack you, fellow.

A hunter saves
    the sparrow
That found shelter
    at his chest.

Walking, standing
    sitting, lying.

The water a cow laps
    turns into milk;
The water a snake licks
    changes into poison.

The vacant sky—
    no front, no back;
The birds' paths—
    no east, no west.

Last year's poverty:
   no land,
      but a gimlet.
This year's—
   no land,
      no gimlet.

To look up
   and never see the sky;
To look down
   and never see the earth.

Walking is Zen;
   sitting, too.

However priceless,
   a piece of gold
In the eye
   is nothing but grit.

Throwing over
  seas and mountains
    look for the one who knows!

Drive off the ox
  from a farmer!
Snatch the food
  from a hungry man!

No one is seen
  deep in the mountain:
Only voices
  resounding....

Emptyhanded come,
  emptyhanded go!

Light
    as a hairtip,
        heavy as a mountain.

The sounds of a valley stream
    wash your ears clean;
The canopy-like pine trees
    touch your eyes green.

No use covering your ears
    —sudden thunder.

Your poems
  like autumn dew,
Wash illusory flowers
  from my eyes.

The moon sets, leaving
  no shadow on the creek;
The clouds come, dressing
    up the mountaintop.

Sweeping leaves by the valley
  in the evening sun
    —a monk.

One rooster's cry
  preaches
    the heaven-and-earth dawn.

Seeing illusion
    but not recognizing it:
It collapses
    of itself.

Watch it and take it
    right now,
Or it's gone
    for a thousand years.

Ride your horse along
    the edge of a sword!
Hide yourself
    in the midst of flames!

To sell dog meat,
    displaying a sheep's head.

Words,
    words, words:
        fluttering drizzle and snow.
Silence,
    silence, silence:
        a roaring thunderbolt.

Words
    fail.
Mind
    fails.

The shimmering lake surface
    charms the kingfishers;
The grass color makes
    the dragonflies drunk.

Chase a fierce tiger,
    riding a blind donkey.

A grass-coat-clad old man
     on a solitary boat
Fishing alone
     in the snowy river.

One roar
     of a lion
Cracks the brains
     of a hundred beasts.

A winter bird shrieks
     on an old tree;
A wild monkey screams
     on an empty mountain.

My mind is
     like the autumn moon:
Shining, bright, reflected
     on the clear creek.

吾心似秋月碧潭清皎潔

Mount Five Plateaus
    claps its hands:
Mount Moth Eyebrows
    laughs.

In front of Lo-yang's
    Five Phoenix Pavilion
        to ask where Lo-yang is.

A good explanation:
    don't explain everything.

A black raven blows off
    the black bucket.

Fragrant winds
    come from the south;
A slight coolness is
    brought into the palace.

Sitting motionless,
    nothing happening—
Spring coming,
    grass growing—

To sense an old temple,
    hearing bell sounds;
To know a hamlet,
    seeing smoke.

No work
    one day,
No food
    that day.

Sit on the mountain rock—
    a cloud rises on your robe.
Scoop water from the spring—
    the moon enters the bottle.

Hands
    grab;
Feet
    walk.

Never leaving
    home: but
        right on the way.
Having left
    home: but
        not on the way.

To fit the shoes
    by cutting the feet;
To fit the crown
    by chipping the head.

At dusk
    rooster cried dawn;
At midnight
    the sun shines bright.

Mountain flowers,
    like brocade;
Valley water brimming,
    indigo.

Mountain huts
    hoard silver:
        a thousand snowy trees.
Fishermen
    own a jewel:
        one grass coat.

Everywhere
    like a burning house.

The carp, having climbed
    the surging Three Waterfalls,
        already a dragon;
Fools still try
    to scoop it up
        from the night pond.

To watch only
    the sharp gimlet
Without seeing
    the square handle.

Cold soup,
    putrid rice:
Even dogs
    won't touch.

Three thousand miles away—
    another one
        who knows.

Impress the paper
    with a seal—
        a sharp, red mark;
Before discussion,
    host and guest
        discerned.

詩向快人吟
酒逢知己飲

Looking
   forward only,
Not knowing how
   to turn back.

Puppets dance
   freely
      on the stage:
Behind them
   the puppeteer
      controls.

Chant poetry
   to your best friend!
Drink wine
   with your true friend!

Three hundred poems
   come to one thing:
"Think
   no evil!"

An errand-boy
　　with a bottle
　　　　buying village wine,
Back home, now
　　dressed up, returns to
　　　　master of the house.

The stink of shit
　　wraps him up.

Hard to realize it's
　　the stink of your own shit!

Ears listen
　　like a deaf man;
Mouths talk
　　like a dumb man.

A pearl stored inside:
    the swamp seems attractive.
A gem hidden somewhere:
    the mountain keeps its glitter.

A carp laughs,
    opening its mouth,
        on a treetop.

Trees show
    the shape of the wind;
Waves blur
    the spirit of the moon.

In the soft mud
    —a thorn.

Buying fish
    directly from the boat—
        it tastes very good;
Treading in the snow
    to buy wine—
        it goes down much better.

A man coming
    to preach yes and no;
Only a
    yes-and-no man.

To waste all day
    in the busy town,
Forgetting the treasure
    in his own house.

Open your hands—
    ten fingertips,
        eight spaces between.

Where ten eyes look—
    where ten fingers point—

A beggar
    boy at
        the crossroads
Hangs from his waist
    an elegant
        bag.

Cries, "I didn't do it!"
    holding the things he stole.

The famous swift horse
    can't catch a mouse
So skillfully
    as a lame kitten.

The green of spring—
    neither high nor low;
The flowering branches—
    some long, some short.

Pines are not straight;
    thorns, not crooked.

Pines are straight;
    thorns, crooked.

Spring sleep—
    hard to notice it's dawn;
Birds already
    chirping here and there.

Everything is true
    just as it is:
Why dislike it?
    Why hate?

Wheat turns
    to butterflies;
Earthworms,
    to lilies.

Wiff after whiff of scent
    from pictured plum blossoms.

No pine has two colors,
    old and new;
The bamboo's knot marks
    up and down.

Angry fists cannot beat
    a smiling face.

Walk forward—
    you'll fall in a pit!
Step back—
    an angry tiger eats your feet!

Magical power,
    marvelous action!
Carrying water,
    shouldering wood.

Where to hide?
    —in a needle's eye.

Watch
    fountain murmur!
Hear
    mountain color!

Only knowing
    a cow gets slender
        but not its horns,
Not knowing
    a man gets enlightened
        and then his phrases.

Turn
    a somersault
        on a needle point.

Waters, however rapid,
    never carry off the moon.

To a man in grief
    the night is long.

The moon by the window:
     always the same,
          just that.
Put plum flowers there,
     and it looks
          different.

Knock on the sky
     and listen to the sound!

Water originally
     contains no sound:
Touching a stone
     makes it murmur.

To push the empty gourd
     along the water.

Heavily drunk,
    lying flat on the sand
        —don't laugh at me—
From the old days,
    very few return
        from the battlefield.

The thousand-foot
    fishing line—
His intention
    is deep in the creek.

The salt
    in the water;
The glue
    in the paints.

Who knows? This
    clear, shallow stream
Runs at last
    to the blue depth of the sea.

Sleep is sweet—
    not knowing the rain
        passed over the mountain,
Now awake to find
    the whole palace
        is cool.

No sharp sword
    can cut it open;
No iron hammer
    strike it out.

Water runs
    back to the ocean;
The moon goes down, but
    never leaves the heavens.

Be master of yourself
    —everywhere:
All you do
    proves true.

Buddha proclaims
    a silent word:
Kasyapa accepts it
    —with a smile.

No other:
    this!

Shattered and split—
    shimmering, dancing—
        the moon on the rapids.

Nothing is wasted
    in a splendid reign.

The iron balance
    bitten by a
        worm.

A clear wind comes
    like an old friend.

Climb barefoot
    a mountain of swords!
Enter the fire
    wearing fur!

The stone man
bows
The bare pillar
claps.

Once you preach,
the point
is gone.

Cutting
    the human
        yes and no,
To live with white clouds
    deep in the mountain,
        the brushwood door shut.

Cry
    after cry
        after cry of joy—
Not minding
    the hair
        turning white.

A butterfly,
    fluttering,
        drills the flowers deep.
A dragonfly,
    darting and hovering,
        dips its tail in the water.

A thousand years,
   a million years,
      darkness all over—
Fills every gutter,
   covers each valley
      —no one understands.

Gingerly, carefully
   look into the abyss;
Walk
   on thin ice.

Easy to gather
   a thousand soldiers;
Hard to get
   one general.

Having preached
   Oneness before,
Now preaches
   Difference.

A good swimmer
    gets drowned;
A good rider
    falls.

In a blink
    it's gone.

To hang a medicine bag
    at the back of the hearse.

Wearing robes,
    eating meals:
Outside of these—
    no Zen.

Curse at one another:
    I'll bring a spare mouth!
Sputter and splutter:
    I'll bring extra spit!

Catch
　　the vigorous horse
　　　of your mind!

Right now, right here:
　　facing each other.

Reach for it, and you'll miss;
　　let it loose, and it'll follow.

To bend a bow
　　after the robber's gone.

Pecking the eggshell
　　from inside and out at once.

Strike the water:
　　a fish's head aches.

A man sticking to a phrase
 —gets lost.

The many-mouthed
 magpie scholar
  finds himself dumb.

Facing each other,
 a thousand miles apart.

The accomplished hermit
 hides in the town;
The immature hermit
 hides in the mountain.

A wide sea lets
 fish hop and leap;
A wide sky allows
 birds to fly and flutter.

The biggest bowl
        fills last.

Great skill looks
        like clumsiness.

A large vessel
        has a large
            life;
A small vessel,
        a small
            living.

The great road
        has no gate;
A thousand crossings
        lead there.

Bamboo shadows sweep
　　the dust on the floor
　　　　—moving nothing.
The moonlight
　　drills a creek
　　　　—leaving no trace.

A thick bamboo bush
　　doesn't hinder
　　　　flowing water.
Does a soaring mountain
　　block
　　　　flying white clouds?

To steal Buddha's money
    and buy incense for him.

Everywhere in Ch'ang-an
    lighter than
        in daylight:
Those guys go
    feeling for the wall
        as if it's midnight.

The patter of rain, a suggestion
    of the cold day's end:
Opening the gate, to find
    many fallen leaves.

A long one is
    the Long Body of Buddha;
A short one,
    the Short Body of Buddha.

Chang
    drinks wine:
        Li gets drunk.

Too long a whip
    can't hit the horse's belly.

Don't make
    a ring
        from a straight tree.
Don't make
    a rafter
        from a crooked one.

Jewels on
    Indra's net
Reflect each other
    endlessly.

To distinguish dragons from snakes,
    black from white:
The very business
    of a true master.

Poisoned wine: one cup
    instantly
        staggers a man.

Washing jewels
    in the mud.

The iron ox
    lays stone eggs.

The day dawns:
    fire gets useless.

Above the heavens,
    below the heavens:
Only I
    am holy.

The eastern mountains
    walk on the waters.

Look up
    —the heavens!
Look down
    —the earth!

Honey on the sword edge,
    poison in the wine.

Coming back with satori
    but everything
        just as before:
Hermit Mountain's
    drizzle and mist,
        Crooked River's waves.

The net-breaking dragon,
    hitting
        against the heavens,
Gripping clouds,
    grabbing fog,
        gone at once.

A praying mantis,
    raising its pincers,
        attacks the armored car.

On the same road,
    different wheel tracks.

A single palm
    makes no sound.

Gulp down
    mountains-rivers-great-earth!

Gulp it down, no good!
    Throw it up, no good!

On the southern mountain,
    drumming: dancing
        on the northern.

From north and south,
    from east and west,
        no road enters it:
Rugged
    iron mountains
        —shooting up.

To light a single lamp
  in broad daylight.

Day after day
  a very good day:
Winds come
  and trees bow.

Day after day, day
    dawns in the east;
Day after day, day's
    done in the west.

Enter a tiger's cave
    and stroke its whiskers!

A blade cuts
    things
        but not itself;
Eyes see
    everything
        but themselves.

In the willow, become green!
    In the flower, become red!

To climb one more floor
　　up the pavilion,
Trying for
　　a thousand-mile view.

A man passing
　　over the bridge
Sees the bridge flowing
　　—not the water.

Life is but
　　a hundred-year dream:
Nevertheless,
　　a thousand-year worry.

Human faces, peach blossoms
　　reflect each other
　　　　bright pink.

Easy to reach
   Nirvana;
Hard to enter
   Difference.

Every year, each year
   flowers bloom
     alike;
Each year, every year
   people
     change.

Farmers sing
   in the field;
Merchants dance
   at the market.

How can you hide
   an auger in a paper bag?

The mirror, shattered,
   reflects never again;
The fallen blossom never
   returns to its twig.

A lame tortoise with
   made-up eyebrows
      stands in the evening breeze.

Wrap a clear wind
   with a torn
      robe.

A no-ear banana,
   hearing thunder roar,
      opens its leaves;
A no-eye sunflower,
   seeing the sun,
      turns its head.

Rain of no sorrow
    falls
        on banana leaves:
A man,
    hearing its pattering,
        feels his heart broken.

Beyond
    the white clouds—
        a blue mountain:
A traveler
    goes
        beyond that mountain.

Don't say
    no one comes
        this far.
These eye-filling
    mountains:
        not your best friends?

I've scooped the valley's
pine winds for you—
Have a sip!

White clouds embrace
the dim rocks.

Scooping the water
to catch waves.

He dies,
I die—
Where can we
meet?

Kingfishers
    shatter the dew
        on the lotus leaves.
While herons
    stir the mist
        in the bamboo bush.

Rich food
    doesn't tempt
        the man who has eaten.

The dim pines ripple
    in a soft wind:
Come closer—
    the whisper is better.

Spring opens
    a hundred flowers
    —for whom?

Inside the eye
   of a flea's flea:
      five Mount Sumerus.

Elbows can't be
   turned outward.

Eyebrows lie
   above the eyes.

On a hundred-foot
   pole top,
      step forward!
Man of freedom
   shows up everywhere
      in the ten directions!

People use it
　　daily,
　　　　not knowing it.

The cloth drum
　　knocking on the eaves:
Anyone
　　know the sound?

Disregarding
   a bright pearl,
Regarding it
   as rubbish.

Guest and host:
   interchangeable.

Guest, host—
   obviously different.

I don't know
   the true face of
      this Hermit Mountain
Because I
   live here
      on it.

Not leaving
   Satan's world,
      enter Buddha's!

Living on the mountain:
   a few steps
      from the gate
Gives a whole landscape
   of hundreds and thousands
      of mountains and rivers.

Without surviving
   this marrow-piercing
      cold,
How can the plum blossoms
   radiate
      nose-hitting fragrance?

Hearing one,
   knowing ten.

The woman shakes her loom,
   rattling, clattering. . .
The baby opens its mouth,
   aaaah, aaaah....

Winds drive
   all the clouds
      off the blue heavens;
On the green mountain
   the moon rises
      —one round pearl.

The winds fallen,
   a flower yet drops;
One bird's cry deepens
   the silence of the mountain.

Winds come
    with fountain's murmur
      to the pillow;
The moon transfers
    the flowers' shadows
      to the window.

Say one word
    with your mouth shut!

Ordinary mind
    is the way.

Casting out
    the gold, to pick
        the broken brick.

Every step, each step
    —the monastery.

At each step,
    the pure wind rises.

Glimpsing a flower
    behind the curtain,
        I ask who—
A smile
    on her colored lips
        —no word.

Hurt yourself
    holding a sword blade!
Who's
    to blame?

Meeting Sakyamuni,
    kill him!
Meeting Bodhidharma,
    kill him, too!

From the origins
    nothing exists.

Under the staff blows,
    seeking satori—
No concession to your roshi
    at that moment.

The ordinary and the sacred
     live together;
Dragons and snakes
     all mixed up.

Worldly passions inseparable
     from satori.

Open your hand,
     it becomes a cloud;
          turn it over, rain.

To beat blindly
     the poison-painted drum.

In Nothing,
    everything is contained:
        limitless—
Flowers,
    moon,
        pavilions.

On the foggy sea:
    the compass pointing south.
On a night trip:
    the North Star.

Watch the North Star,
    your face to the south.

Ceaseless
    worries
        of my mind:
One evening's
    talk
        unburdens it.

The clear mirror,
    seeing the object,
Instantly discerns
    the beautiful and the ugly.

Under the fierce tiger's jaw
    —a golden bell!
In the blue dragon's cave
    —a bright pearl!

On his face,
    oleander flowers;
In his heart,
    thorns.

A fierce tiger paints
    coquettish eyebrows.

庸他痴聖
人担雪共
填井

Lie down in front
    of an angry tiger's mouth!
Scratch where it itches
    while on a venomous snake!

Asking for the east,
    to be told, "There's the west!"

The night's so quiet:
    valley murmur closer—
The garden's so cold:
    moon color brighter—

Hiring another
    holy idiot,
Trying to fill up the old well
    with the snow they're carrying.

A donkey matter's
    unsolved but—
A horse problem's
    already come.

To walk in the dark
    in one's best clothes.

The two mirrors
    reflect each other.

A skilled craftsman has
    no material to waste;
A bright king has
    no attendant to dismiss.

Good medicine
   tastes bitter
      —works well;
Frank advice
   sounds irritating
      —helps a lot.

A donkey's dung—
   comparable to jasmine?

The sacred tortoise
   clumps over the land:
How can it erase
   a trail in the dirt?

If you meet on the way
   a man who knows,
Don't speak a word,
   —don't keep silent!

Old age deepens
   the love
      of mountain life.
Dying by the cliffside:
   my bones
      will be clean.

COMPANIONS FOR THE JOURNEY SERIES

This series presents inspirational work by well-known writers
in a small-book format designed to be carried along
on your journey through life.

Volume 6
A Zen Forest: Zen Sayings
Translated by Soioku Shigematsu
Preface by Gary Snyder
1-893996-30-1   5 x 7   140 pages $14.00

Volume 5
Back Roads to Far Towns
Basho's Travel Journal
Translated by Cid Corman
1-893996-31-X   5 x 7   128 pages $13.00

Volume 4
Heaven My Blanket, Earth My Pillow
Poems from Sung Dynasty China by Yang Wan-Li
Translated by Jonathan Chaves
1-893996-29-8   5 x 7   120 pages $14.00

Volume 3
10,000 Dawns
The Love Poems of Claire and Yvan Goll
Translated by Thomas Rain Crowe and Nan Watkins
1-893996-27-1   5 x 7   96 pages $13.00

Volume 2
There Is No Road
Proverbs by Antonio Machado
Translated by Mary G. Berg & Dennis Maloney
1-893996-66-2   5 x 7   120 pages $14.00

Volume I
Wild Ways: Zen Poems of Ikkyu
Translated by John Stevens
1-893996-65-4   5 x 7   128 pages $14.00

www.ingramcontent.com/pod-product-compliance
Lightning Source LLC
Jackson TN
JSHW080852211224
75817JS00002B/19

9781893996304